NATIONAL GEOGRAPHIC

Electricity at Home

USING ELECTRICITY

Rita Mullick

D0613510

PICTURE CREDITS

Cover: teenage girl lying on the bed with a laptop, Photodisc.

Page 1, Image Source; page 4 (left), Digital Vision; page 4 (right), Banana Stock; page 5 (top) © Denis Felix/Taxi/Getty Images; page 5 (bottom left), Stockdisc Classic; page 5 (bottom right), Emrah Turudu/iStockphoto.com; page 6, Digital Vision; pages 7–8 © Kevin Currie; page 9 © Macmillan Education Australia; page 11 © Kevin Currie; page 12 © Todd Warnock/Stone/Getty Images; page 13 © Photolibrary; page 14 (top), fStop; page 14 (bottom) © Tom Fowlks/Stone+/Getty Images; page 15 © Kevin Currie; page 16 (left), Corbis; page 16 (middle & right) © Macmillan Education Australia; page 19 (top, bottom middle, bottom second from right), Photodisc; page 19 (middle, bottom left, bottom right) © Macmillan Education Australia; page 19 (bottom second from left), shutterstock.com; pages 21–26 © Alan Laver; page 29, Digital Vision.

Produced through the worldwide resources of the National Geographic Society, John M. Fahey, Jr., President and Chief Executive Officer; Gilbert M. Grosvenor, Chairman of the Board.

PREPARED BY NATIONAL GEOGRAPHIC SCHOOL PUBLISHING
Sheron Long, Chief Executive Officer; Samuel Gesumaria, President; Steve Mico, Executive Vice President and Publisher; Francis Downey, Editor in Chief; Richard Easby, Editorial Manager; Margaret Sidlosky, Director of Design and Illustrations; Jim Hiscott, Design Manager; Cynthia Olson and Ruth Ann Thompson, Art Directors; Matt Wascavage, Director of Publishing Services; Lisa Pergolizzi, Production Manager.

MANUFACTURING AND QUALITY CONTROL
Christopher A. Liedel, Chief Financial Officer; Phillip L. Schlosser, Vice President; Clifton M. Brown III, Director.

EDITOR
Mary Anne Wengel

PROGRAM CONSULTANTS
Dr. Shirley V. Dickson, National Literacy Consultant; James A. Shymansky, E. Desmond Lee Professor of Science Education, University of Missouri-St Louis.

National Geographic Theme Sets program developed by Macmillan Science and Education Australia Pty Limited.

Copyright © 2007 National Geographic Society.
All Rights Reserved. Reproduction of the whole or any part of the contents without written permission from the publisher is prohibited. National Geographic, National Geographic School Publishing, and the Yellow Border are registered trademarks of the National Geographic Society.

Published by the National Geographic Society
1145 17th Street N.W.
Washington, D.C. 20036-4688

ISBN: 978-1-4263-5155-6

Printed in China by The Central Printing (Hong Kong) Ltd.
Quarry Bay, Hong Kong
Supplier Code: OCP May 2018
Macmillan Job: 804263
Cengage US PO: 15308030

MEA10_May18_S

Contents

Using Electricity

Electricity is a form of energy. People use electricity to power many things, from light bulbs to big machines. People use electricity everywhere. They use it at home, at play, at school, and at work.

Key Concepts

1. Electricity involves the movement of electrons.
2. An electric circuit is a path along which electrons can move.
3. Electric energy can change to heat, light, sound, and movement.

Where Electricity Is Used

At Home

Appliances at home need electricity to work.

At Play

Some play equipment needs electricity to work.

In this book you will learn how electricity is used at home.

At School

Some school equipment needs electricity to work.

At Work

Most office and factory equipment needs electricity to work.

Using Electricity at Home

Did you turn on a light at home today? Did you cook food or take a shower? If you did, you may have used electricity. People use electricity in many ways in the home. What would your day be like without electricity? You would not be able to use lights, ovens, or toasters.

Key Concept 1 Electricity involves the movement of electrons.

Parts of an Atom

Everything on Earth is made up of particles called **atoms.** Atoms are tiny. You cannot see them with your eyes. You can only see them with a special microscope. A speck of dust is made up of billions of atoms.

These pieces of metal are made up of billions of atoms.

Each atom is made up of smaller particles.
They are called protons, neutrons, and
electrons. Protons and neutrons make up the
center of an atom. Electrons move around them.

electrons
particles that
move around the
center of an atom

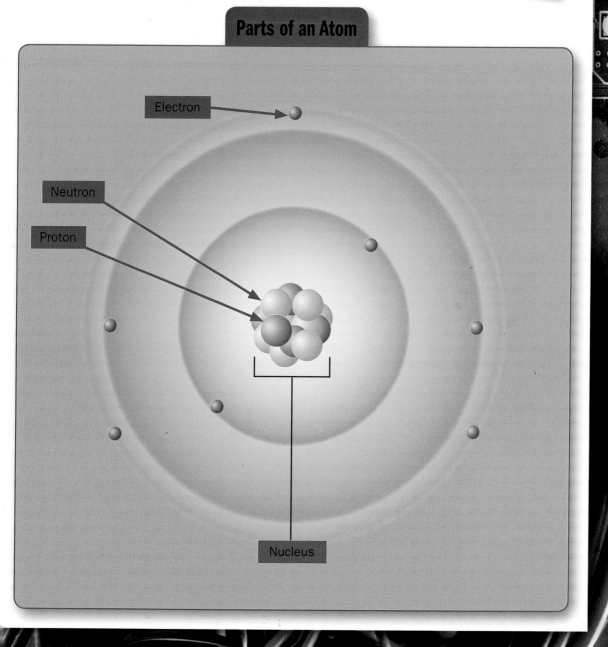

Parts of an Atom

Electron

Neutron

Proton

Nucleus

Electrons and Electricity

Electrons move around the center of an atom. They also move from atom to atom. The flow of electrons is called an **electric current.** Moving electrons have energy. This energy is called **electricity.**

An electric current flows through wires to your home. Electricity makes things in your home work. It heats a toaster to make toast. It makes light bulbs light up so you can see.

electricity
the energy of moving electrons

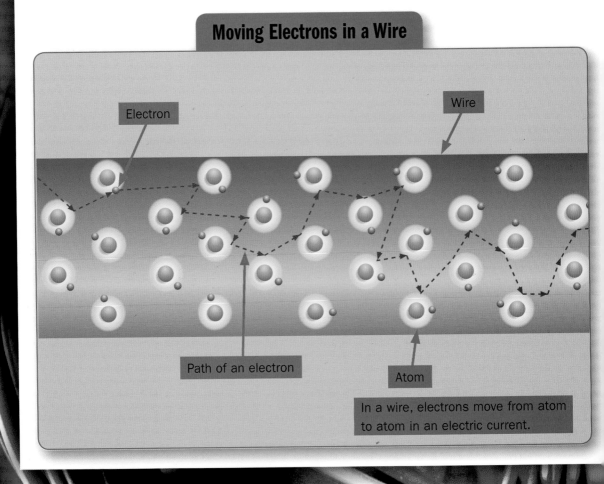

Moving Electrons in a Wire

Electron

Wire

Path of an electron

Atom

In a wire, electrons move from atom to atom in an electric current.

Conductors and Insulators

Electrons move easily through **conductors.** Metals are good conductors. Copper is a metal. Wire is often made of copper.

Electrons do not move easily through **insulators.** Plastic and rubber are good insulators. Wires in your home are covered with plastic. The plastic is the insulator. The plastic makes wires safe to touch. It protects you from the electricity in the wires.

Copper is used as a conductor in circuit boards.

Insulated Wire

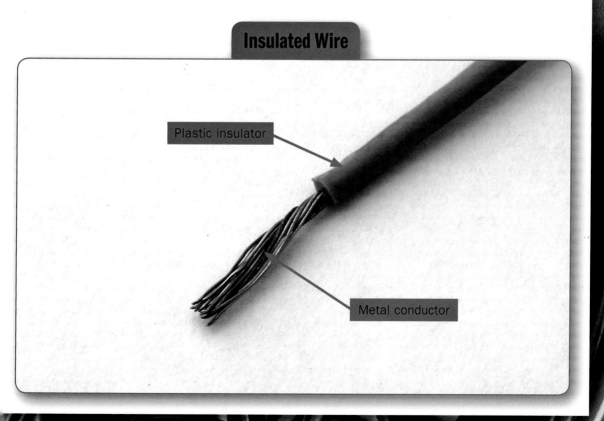

Plastic insulator

Metal conductor

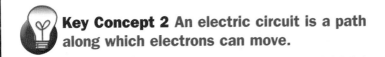

Key Concept 2 An electric circuit is a path along which electrons can move.

Electric Circuits

An electric current flows in a path called a **circuit.** A circuit may be closed or open.

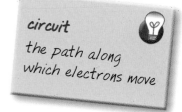

circuit

the path along which electrons move

An electric current flows in a closed circuit. It flows from a power source to an appliance in a loop. Electricity makes the appliance work. It only works if there is no gap in the loop.

A circuit with a gap in it is called an open circuit. The gap stops the current from reaching the appliance. The appliance does not work. A switch closes or opens the circuit. It turns the appliance on or off.

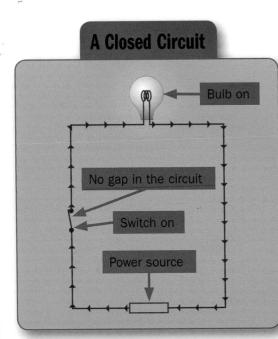

A Closed Circuit

Bulb on

No gap in the circuit

Switch on

Power source

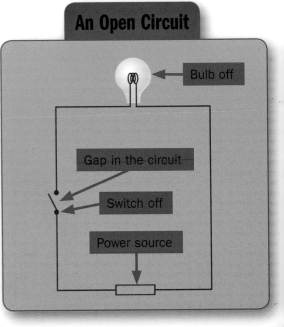

An Open Circuit

Bulb off

Gap in the circuit

Switch off

Power source

The Circuit of a Light Bulb

A lamp in your home is part of a circuit. When you turn on the lamp, you close the circuit. Electricity makes the light bulb give off light. When you turn off the lamp, you open the circuit. The electric current does not reach the light bulb. The light bulb does not give off light.

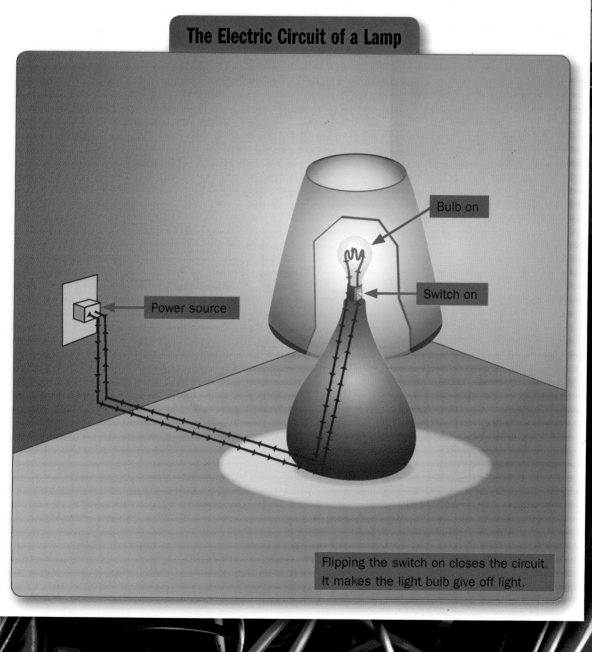

The Electric Circuit of a Lamp

Bulb on

Switch on

Power source

Flipping the switch on closes the circuit. It makes the light bulb give off light.

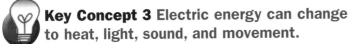

Using Electricity at Home

Electricity enters your home through wires. At home, appliances change electric energy. They change it to other forms of energy. Some of these forms of energy are heat, light, sound, and movement.

Wires bring electricity to homes. The electricity makes home appliances work.

Changing Electric Energy to Heat Energy

Some appliances change electric energy to heat energy. A toaster changes electric energy to heat energy. Electricity moves through the wires inside a toaster. The wires are very thin. Electrons move less freely in thin wires. The slowing down of electrons is called **resistance.** Resistance makes electrons bump into each other. As they bump into each other, they give off heat.

In the toaster, the thin wires get so hot that they glow. The heat energy dries the bread and toasts it.

The wires in a toaster heat up when an electric current flows through them.

Changing Electric Energy to Light Energy

Some devices change electric energy to light energy. A light bulb has a **filament.** An electric current flows through the filament when you turn on the light. The filament has high resistance like the wires inside a toaster. The resistance heats up the filament. It glows and gives off light.

When the filament in a bulb gets hot, it gives off light.

Filament

Bulbs light up lamps at home.

Changing Electric Energy to Sound Energy

Some devices change electric energy to sound energy. An electric doorbell uses electric energy to make sound.

When you push a doorbell button, you close a circuit. The electricity in the circuit activates an **electromagnet.** The electromagnet attracts a metal clapper. The clapper then strikes the bell. If you keep pushing the button, the bell keeps ringing.

How a Doorbell Works

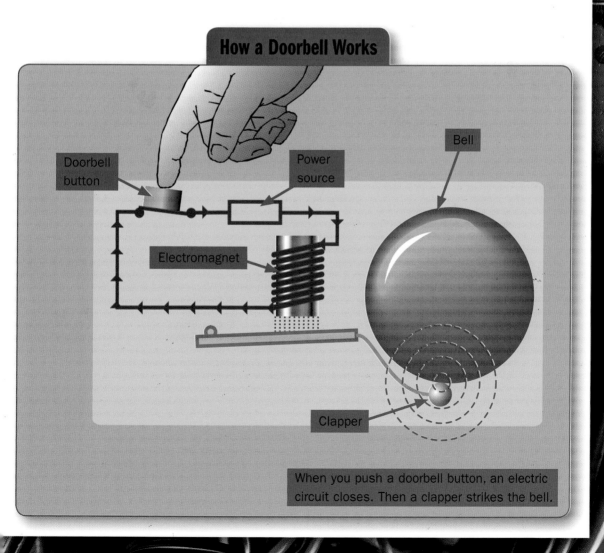

Doorbell button

Power source

Bell

Electromagnet

Clapper

When you push a doorbell button, an electric circuit closes. Then a clapper strikes the bell.

Changing Electric Energy to Movement

Electric energy can also change to movement. This movement is called **mechanical energy.** Some appliances have a part called a motor. A washing machine has a motor. Vacuum cleaners and ceiling fans have motors. Electricity makes a part in the motor move. A blender has a motor. The motor makes the blade turn. The turning blade makes a great milkshake.

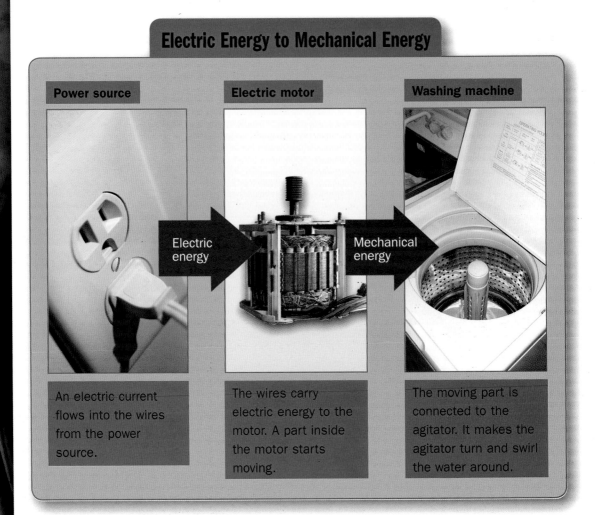

Electric Energy to Mechanical Energy

Power source

Electric motor

Washing machine

Electric energy

Mechanical energy

An electric current flows into the wires from the power source.

The wires carry electric energy to the motor. A part inside the motor starts moving.

The moving part is connected to the agitator. It makes the agitator turn and swirl the water around.

Think About the **Key Concepts**

Think about what you read. Think about the pictures and diagrams. Use them to answer the questions. Share what you think with others.

1. What is electricity? What do electrons have to do with electricity?

2. How are conductors and insulators used together?

3. What does a switch do in an electric circuit?

4. What other forms of energy can electric energy change to?

Flow Diagram

Diagrams use pictures and words to explain ideas.
You can learn new ideas without having to read a lot of words.

There are different kinds of diagrams.
The diagram on page 19 is a flow diagram. It shows how electricity gets to your home. A flow diagram uses pictures and captions to show how something takes place. It shows the steps in a process. Look back at the diagram on page 16. It is a flow diagram of how electric energy changes to mechanical energy.

How to Read a Diagram

1. Read the title.
It tells you what the diagram is about.

2. Read the labels or captions.
They tell you about the parts of the diagram.

3. Study the pictures.
Pictures help show the steps. The arrows are pictures too. They show the order of the steps.

4. Think about what you learned.
Decide what new information you learned from the diagram.

From the Power Station to the Home

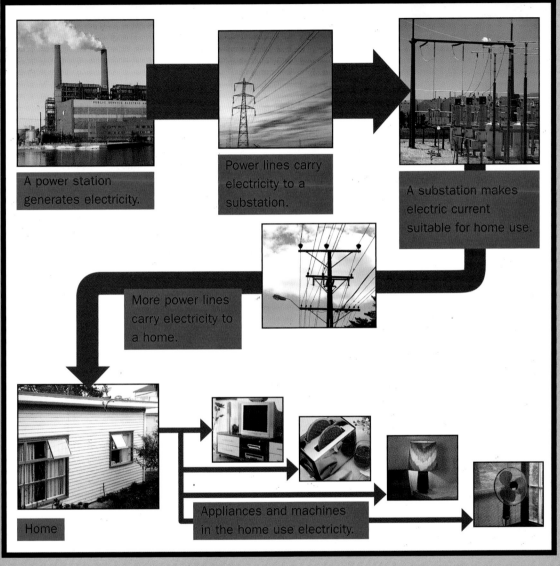

A power station generates electricity.

Power lines carry electricity to a substation.

A substation makes electric current suitable for home use.

More power lines carry electricity to a home.

Home

Appliances and machines in the home use electricity.

Follow the Arrows

Read the diagram by following the steps on page 18. Write down what you learned about how electricity gets to your home. Where is electricity generated? What does electricity flow through? How is electricity used in your home? Explain the process to a classmate.

How-to Books

The purpose of how-to books is to give directions. How-to books take many forms.

Cookbook

Craft Book

Exercise Manual

How-to Books

How to...

User Manual

Gardening Guide

You use different how-to books to find out how to make or do something. If you want to know how to use an appliance, you read a user manual. User manuals come with appliances when you buy them.

User manuals give you all the information you need to know before you use an appliance. They tell you how to operate the appliance. They also tell you how to care for the appliance and how to use it safely.

Toaster User Manual

The **title** tells which appliance the user manual is for.

Congratulations on buying a new toaster. Read the user manual before you use the toaster. The manual will tell you how to use your toaster.

Parts of the Toaster

Subheads break the information into easy-to-find sections.

A Controls

B Knob

C Power cord

D Crumb tray

E Browning control

F Bread slots

Labels show the parts of the appliance.

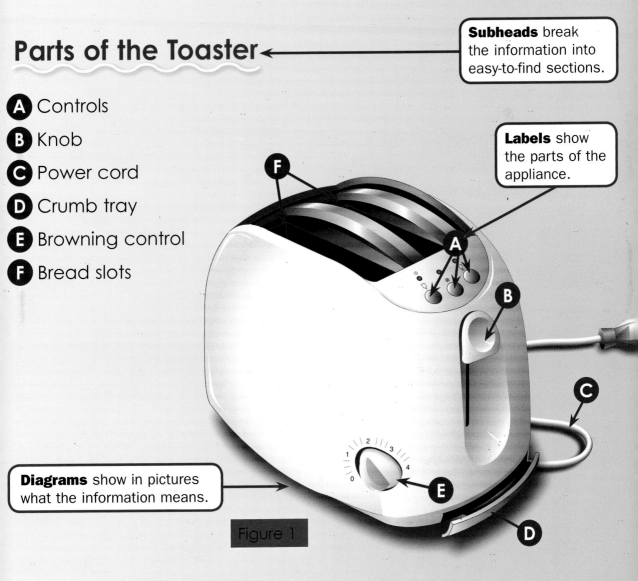

Diagrams show in pictures what the information means.

Figure 1

Safety Measures

Take care when using your toaster. Follow the instructions below for safe use.

⚠ Unplug the toaster when you are not using it.

⚠ Be careful when you touch the toaster. Some parts of the toaster will be hot after use.

⚠ Do not allow your toaster or its cord to get wet. (Figure 2)

⚠ Do not use your toaster in closed places, such as cupboards.

⚠ Do not use your toaster on hot surfaces, such as stove tops. Hot surfaces can damage the power cord.

⚠ Never put a metal object into the toaster. (Figure 3)

⚠ Do not use your toaster near drapes. (Figure 4)

Important information is presented in bulleted lists so it is easy to find and read.

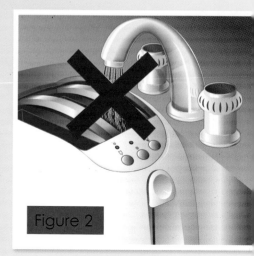
Figure 2

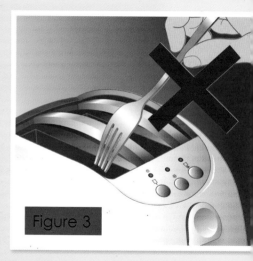
Figure 3

Figure 4

Setting Up the Toaster

- Carefully unpack the toaster.

- Check the toaster for any damage. If there is damage, return the toaster to the store.

- Make sure the knob moves up and down. (Figure 5)

- Make sure the crumb tray moves in and out. (Figure 6)

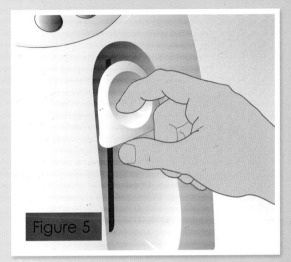

Figure 5

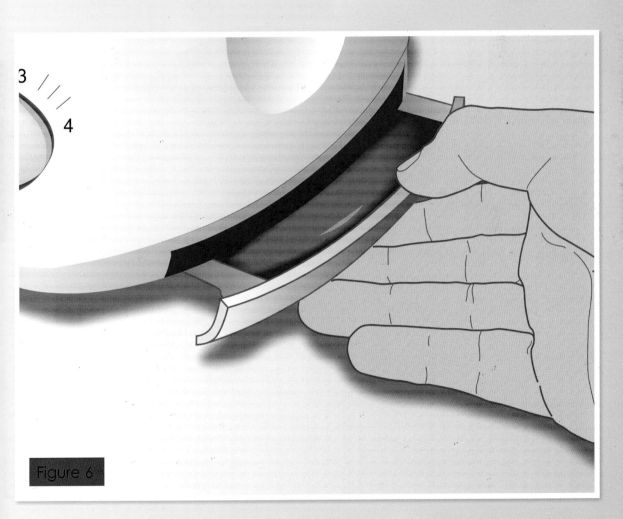

3

4

Figure 6

Using the Toaster

Toasting

- Plug the cord into the power source.

- Turn the browning control to the level you want. The higher you set it, the browner your toast will be. (Figure 7)

- Place slices of bread in the bread slots. Press the knob down. The toast will pop up when it is done.

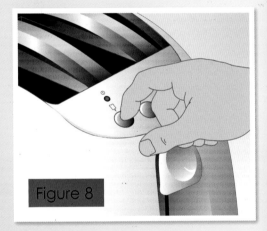

Figure 7

Reheating

- To reheat cold toast, put the toast into the bread slots. Press the knob down. Press the reheat button. (Figure 8)

Defrosting

- To toast frozen bread, put the frozen bread into the bread slots. Press the knob down. Press the defrost button. (Figure 9)

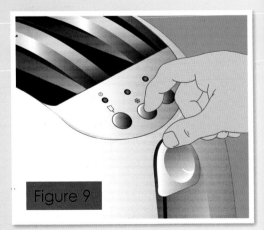

Figure 8

Figure 9

Troubleshooting

This is the troubleshooting, or problem-solving, section.
Use this section if you have a problem with the toaster.

The Toaster Does Not Heat Up
- Make sure the plug is inserted into the power source. (Figure 10)

- Make sure the knob is pressed down.

The Toaster Does Not Brown the Bread
- Make sure you have the toaster set on the correct browning setting. (Figure 11)

If the toaster still does not work, contact the store.

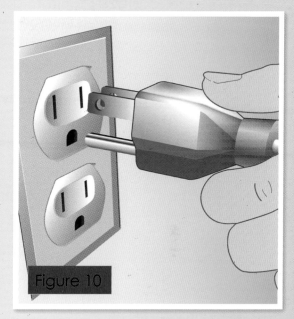

Figure 10

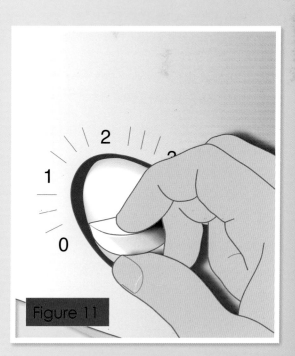

Figure 11

Caring for the Toaster

Storing

- Store the toaster and its cord in a clean, dry place.

- Store the toaster away from sharp kitchen tools, such as knives.

Cleaning

- Unplug the toaster.

- Do not put any part of the toaster in water.

- Wipe the outer surface with a damp cloth. Dry with a towel. (Figure 12)

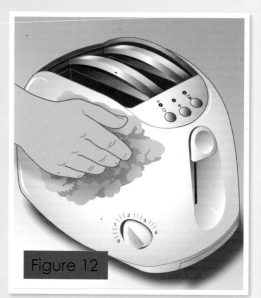

Figure 12

Emptying the Crumb Tray

If you use the toaster daily, you should empty the crumb tray each week.

- Make sure the toaster has fully cooled. Unplug it.

- Pull out the crumb tray. Throw away the crumbs. (Figure 13)

- Replace the crumb tray.

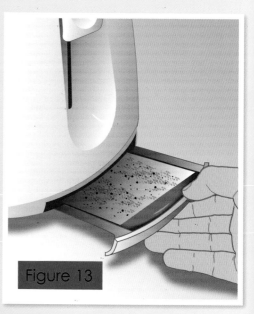

Figure 13

Apply the **Key Concepts**

Key Concept 1 Electricity involves the movement of electrons.

Activity

Think about what you know about electrons. What are electrons? Can you see electrons with your eyes? What do electrons have to do with electricity? Draw a word web showing what you know about electrons.

move

Electrons

Key Concept 2 An electric circuit is a path along which electrons can move.

Activity

Look around you. Name four objects that are part of an electric circuit. Choose one and draw a circuit for that object. Label the parts of the circuit.

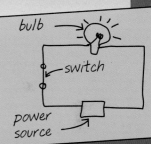

bulb

switch

power source

Key Concept 3 Electric energy can change to heat, light, sound, and movement.

Activity

Write a paragraph or two about something you used today that uses electricity. Did it change electric energy into another kind of energy? How was that useful to you?

I turned on the TV. . . .

Write
Your Own
User Manual

You have read the user manual for the toaster. Now think of a different appliance you use at home. Write a user manual for it.

1. Study the Model

Look back at the user manual on pages 21–26. What information is presented under each section? How do bulleted lists make the information easy to find and read? How do diagrams help you understand the information in the user manual?

2. Choose an Appliance

Choose an appliance you use at home. Make notes on what the appliance does and how it operates. Think about how it should be used safely. How should you clean and take care of the appliance? What should you do if something goes wrong with the appliance?

User Manual
- Break the information into easy-to-find sections.
- Present the information in bulleted lists.
- Use diagrams to support the text.
- Include important safety measures.

3. Write a User Manual

Use subheads that are similar to the ones in the toaster user manual. Present the important information clearly in bulleted lists under the subheads. Try to make your information and instructions easy to follow and understand.

4. Draw Diagrams

Draw a diagram and label the different parts of your appliance. Then draw smaller diagrams to help illustrate the information in your bulleted lists.

5. Read over Your Work

Read over your user manual, correcting any spelling mistakes or punctuation errors. Make sure your user manual is easy to understand. Are your instructions for use easy to follow? Do your diagrams clearly illustrate the text? Have you listed all the safety measures? Did you describe how to care for the appliance? Is there any other information the user of the appliance might need to know?

Safety Measures

- Never use the appliance near water.

- Unplug the appliance after use.

- Keep the appliance out of the reach of children.

Present Your User Manual

Now that you have chosen an appliance and written a user manual for it, you can present your user manual to the rest of the class.

How to Present Your User Manual

1. Copy your labeled diagram onto an overhead transparency.
Draw the diagram clearly so you can show the different parts of your appliance to the class.

2. Explain your appliance to the class.
Take turns presenting your appliances and machines in class. Show the class the different parts of your appliance on the overhead projector. Explain to the class what the appliance is used for and how the appliance works.

3. Explain the safety measures.
It is important to follow the safety measures carefully when you use any appliance. Tell the class of any possible dangers with using your appliance. Explain how to use the appliance in the safest way possible.

4. Show the class how to care for the appliance.
Tell the class how to clean, store, and care for the parts of your appliance to keep it in the best working order.

Glossary

atoms – tiny particles that make up matter

circuit – the path along which electrons move

conductors – materials through which an electric current moves easily

electric current – the movement of electrons

electricity – the energy of moving electrons

electromagnet – a piece of metal that becomes a magnet when an electric current passes through a wire wound around it

electrons – particles that move around the center of an atom

filament – a wire that glows when heated by an electric current

insulators – materials through which an electric current moves with difficulty

mechanical energy – the energy of movement or moving parts

resistance – slowing down the flow of electrons

Index